HSE

First aid at work 14 Day Loan

The Health and Safety (First-Aid) Regulations 1981

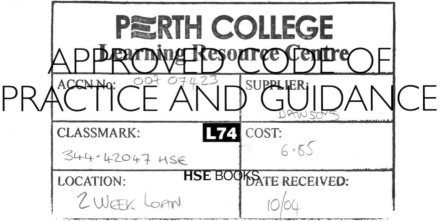

APPROVED CODE OF PRACTICE AND GUIDANCE

Both the Code and guidance in this publication give
advice on how to comply with the Regulations, but there
is an important distinction between them:

This Code has been approved by the Health and Safety
Commission, with the consent of the Secretary of State.
It gives practical advice on how to comply with the law.
If you follow the advice you will be doing enough to
comply with the law in respect of those specific matters
on which the Code gives advice. You may use alternative
methods to those set out in the Code in order to comply
with the law.

However, the Code has a special legal status. If you are
prosecuted for breach of health and safety law, and it is
proved that you did not follow the relevant provisions of
the Code, you will need to show that you have complied
with the law in some other way or a Court will find you
at fault.

This guidance is issued by the Health and Safety
Executive. Following the guidance is not compulsory and
you are free to take other action. But if you do follow the
guidance you will normally be doing enough to comply
with the law. Health and safety inspectors seek to secure
compliance with the law and may refer to this guidance
as illustrating good practice.

Contents

By virtue of section 16(4) of the Health and Safety at Work etc Act 1974 and with the consent of the Secretary of State for the Environment, the Health and Safety Commission has on 29 January 1997 approved the revised Code of Practice entitled *First Aid at Work*.

The revised Approved Code of Practice gives practical guidance with respect to the Health and Safety (First-Aid) Regulations 1981 (SI 1981 No 917).

The revised Approved Code of Practice comes into effect on 14 March 1997 and on that date the 1990 edition of the Code of Practice shall cease to have effect.

Signed

T A GATES
Secretary to the Health and Safety Commission

29 January 1997

1   The Health and Safety (First-Aid) Regulations 1981 set out the essential aspects of first aid that employers have to address. This publication has been prepared to help employers understand and comply with the Regulations and offers practical and realistic advice on what employers might do. Practical guidance on first aid in mines is given in a separate publication[1].

2   This publication contains the Regulations themselves, an Approved Code of Practice and guidance. Paragraphs are marked to indicate which these are as follows:

Regulation

Approved Code of Practice

Guidance

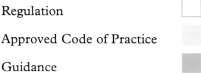

Regulation 1

Citation and commencement

These Regulations may be cited as the Health and Safety (First-Aid) Regulations 1981 and shall come into operation on 1st July 1982.

Regulation 2

Interpretation

(1)   In these Regulations, unless the context otherwise requires -

"first-aid" means -

(a)   in cases where a person will need help from a medical practitioner or nurse, treatment for the purpose of preserving life and minimising the consequences of injury and illness until such help is obtained, and

(b)   treatment of minor injuries which would otherwise receive no treatment or which do not need treatment by a medical practitioner or nurse;

"mine" means a mine within the meaning of Section 180 of the Mines and Quarries Act 1954[(a)].

(2)   In these Regulations, unless the context otherwise requires, any reference to -

(a)   a numbered Regulation or Schedule is a reference to the Regulation of, or Schedule to, these Regulations bearing that number;

(b)   a numbered paragraph is a reference to the paragraph bearing that number in the Regulation in which the reference appears.

(a)   1954 c.70; relevant amending instrument is SI 1974/2013.

Definition of first aid

3   People at work can suffer injuries or fall ill. It doesn't matter whether the injury or illness is caused by the work they do. It is important that they receive immediate attention and that an ambulance is called in serious cases. First aid can save lives and prevent minor injuries becoming major ones. First aid at work covers the arrangements that need to be made to ensure this happens, that is, the initial management of any injury or illness suffered at work. It does not include giving tablets or medicines to treat illness. The Regulations do not prevent staff who are specially trained to take action beyond the initial management stage from doing so.

Duty of employer to make provision for first-aid

(1)   An employer shall provide, or ensure that there are provided, such equipment and facilities as are adequate and appropriate in the circumstances for enabling first-aid to be rendered to his employees if they are injured or become ill at work.

(2)   Subject to paragraphs (3) and (4), an employer shall provide, or ensure that there is provided, such number of suitable persons as is adequate and appropriate in the circumstances for rendering first-aid to his employees if they are injured or become ill at work; and for this purpose a person shall not be suitable unless he has undergone -

(a)   such training and has such qualifications as the Health and Safety Executive may approve for the time being in respect of that case or class of case, and

(b)   such additional training, if any, as may be appropriate in the circumstances of that case.

(3)   Where a person provided under paragraph (2) is absent in temporary and exceptional circumstances it shall be sufficient compliance with that paragraph if the employer appoints a person, or ensures that a person is appointed, to take charge of -

(a)   the situation relating to an injured or ill employee who will need help from a medical practitioner or nurse, and

(b)   the equipment and facilities provided under paragraph (1)

throughout the period of any such absence.

(4)   Where having regard to -

(a)   the nature of the undertaking, and

(b)   the number of employees at work, and

(c)   the location of the establishment,

it would be adequate and appropriate if instead of a person for rendering first-aid there was a person appointed to take charge as in paragraph (3) (a) and (b), then instead of complying with paragraph (2) the employer may appoint such a person, or ensure that such a person is appointed.

Assessment of need

4   An employer should make an assessment of first-aid needs appropriate to the circumstances of each workplace.

5   The aim of first aid is to reduce the effects of injury or illness suffered at work, either caused by the work itself or by some factor outside the employer's control. First-aid provision must be 'adequate and appropriate in the circumstances'. This means that sufficient first-aid personnel and facilities should be available:

● to give immediate assistance to casualties with both common injuries or illness and those likely to arise from specific hazards at work;

● to summon an ambulance or other professional help.

6   How much first-aid provision an employer has to make depends on the circumstances in each workplace. No fixed level exists but each employer needs to assess what facilities and personnel are appropriate. Where employers have an occupational health service or access to other occupational health advice, they might wish to delegate the responsibility for carrying out the assessment and advising on first-aid provision to that service or source of advice.

7   The training and experience of:

● qualified medical doctors registered with the General Medical Council; and

● nurses whose names are registered in Parts 12, 13, 14 and 15 of the Single Professional Register maintained by the United Kingdom Central Council for Nursing, Midwifery and Health Visiting

qualify them to administer first aid. Where such doctors and nurses are employed the employer may take that into account in determining first-aid provision and in particular the need for appointing first aiders.

8   Employers may need to justify on what grounds the level of first-aid provision has been set. Although there is no requirement for the assessment of first-aid needs to be formal or written, it may be useful for employers to record the results.

9   In assessing need, employers need to consider:

● workplace hazards and risks;

● the size of the organisation;

● the organisation's history of accidents;

● the nature and distribution of the workforce;

● the remoteness of the site from emergency medical services;

● the needs of travelling, remote and lone workers;

● employees working on shared or multi-occupied sites;

● annual leave and other absences of first aiders and appointed persons.

Appendix 1 contains a checklist to help employers assess their first-aid needs.

Nature of the work

10   The Management of Health and Safety at Work Regulations 1999 require employers to make a suitable and sufficient assessment of the risks to health and safety of their employees at work to identify what measures they need to take to prevent or control these risks[2,3]. The information gathered from the risk assessment can help the employer to carry out the assessment of first-aid needs if control measures fail. Identifying the likely nature of the accident or injury will help the employer to work out the most appropriate type, quantity and location of first-aid facilities and personnel.

11   In organisations where the risk assessment identifies a comparatively low risk to health and safety, employers may only need to provide a clearly identified and suitably stocked first-aid container (see paragraphs 29-33) and

an appointed person to look after first-aid arrangements and take charge in emergencies (see paragraphs 58-61).

12   However, where the work involves particular risks, for example work with hazardous substances or with dangerous tools or machinery, first-aid needs will be greater. Employers may need to:

●   provide a sufficient number of first aiders so that someone is always available to give first aid immediately following an incident (see paragraphs 44-55);

●   train first aiders in special procedures (see paragraph 50);

●   inform the local emergency services, in writing, of the site where hazardous substances or processes are in use;

●   provide first-aid room(s) (see paragraphs 38-43).

13   In making first-aid provision employers will need to take account of the different risks in different parts of the establishment. For example, it is likely that, because of the variety of work carried out, separate risk assessments will have to be made for individual buildings or departments within a University complex. The results of these separate assessments need to be carried over in the assessment of first-aid needs. This will mean that greater provision of first-aid equipment, facilities and personnel will be needed in buildings with higher risk activities than in those with lower risk activities. It would not be appropriate to do a generic assessment of needs to cover a variety of activities.

Size of the organisation

14   Generally the larger the workforce, the more first-aid provision is needed. However, employee numbers should never be the sole basis for determining first-aid needs; there may be greater risks when fewer people are at work, for example during maintenance. Employers should provide sufficient cover for the various circumstances that can occur.

Past history and consequences of accidents

15   In carrying out their assessment of first-aid needs, employers may find it useful to examine the number, type, frequency and consequences of accidents that have occurred in the past. For large multi-site organisations this information could be helpful in determining what first-aid materials and equipment are necessary, where first aiders should be located and what geographical area they should be required to cover.

The nature and distribution of the workforce

16   The particular needs of employees potentially at greater risk, for example young workers, trainees and some people with disabilities, will need to be addressed both as a group and as individuals.

17   An employer should consider how the size of the premises could affect quick access to first-aid facilities, for example whether additional first-aid provision is needed on a site with more than one building, or whether the distance between buildings is such that additional provision would be unnecessary. Employers with a multi-floor building should consider how many first aiders or appointed persons will be required to give adequate provision to each floor.

18   The level of provision for first aid may need to vary where employees work in self-contained areas or where they work shifts. It is important that sufficient first-aid provision is always available when employees are at work, and separate arrangements may have to be made for each area of work or shift.

The remoteness of the site from emergency medical services

19   Where a site is remote from emergency medical services, employers may need to make special arrangements to ensure appropriate transport is available. At the least employers should inform the local emergency services in writing of their location and any particular circumstances including specific hazards.

The needs of travelling, remote and lone workers

20   Employers are responsible for meeting the first-aid needs of their employees working away from the main site, for example those who travel regularly or who work elsewhere. The assessment should determine whether those who travel long distances or are continuously mobile should carry a personal first-aid kit. Organisations with employees who work in remote areas should consider making special arrangements such as issuing personal communicators, providing special training and organising emergency transport facilities. Where employees work alone, other means of summoning help such as a portable telephone may be useful to call for assistance in an emergency.

Employees working on shared or multi-occupied sites

21   On a shared or multi-occupied site, employers can arrange for one employer to take responsibility for providing first-aid cover for all the workers. In these cases, a full exchange of information about the risks and hazards involved should help to make sure that the shared provision is suitable and sufficient. All employers should agree the arrangements and employees should be kept informed. A written agreement between employers is strongly recommended as the best way to avoid misunderstandings.

22   Similarly, where an employment business contracts out employees to another employer, the employment business should ensure, by arrangement with the user employer, that these employees have access to first-aid provision.

Annual leave and other absences of first aiders

23   It is essential that adequate provision is made at all times that people are at work. Employers therefore need to make provision to cover annual leave and other planned absences of first aiders or appointed persons. Employers should also consider what cover is needed for unplanned and exceptional absences such as sick leave or special leave due to bereavement.

Other relevant factors

24   *Trainees.* Trainees undertaking work experience on certain training schemes have the same status as employees for the purposes of health and safety legislation[4]. Employers providing such training are responsible for ensuring adequate first-aid cover for trainees.

25   *The public.* These Regulations do not oblige employers to provide for first aid for anyone other than their own employees. Indeed, Regulations requiring first-aid provision for members of the public cannot be made under the Health and Safety at Work etc Act 1974. But many undertakings, for example educational establishments, health authority premises, places of entertainment, fairgrounds and shops provide a service for others, and employers may wish to

5

include them in their assessment of needs and make provision for them. Employers should be aware that the compulsory element of employers' liability insurance does not cover litigation resulting from first aid to non-employees. However, many public liability insurance policies do cover this aspect and employers may wish to check their public liability insurance policy on this point.

26   Where first-aid provision is intended to cover both employees and others, employers should take care to ensure that the level of provision for:

● employees does not fall below the standard required by these Regulations;

● the public and others complies with other relevant legislation and guidance. For example, the Road Traffic Act 1960 regulates first-aid provision on buses and coaches.

Re-assessment of first-aid provision

27   Employers should review their first-aid needs from time to time, particularly after any operating changes, to ensure that the provision remains appropriate.

First-aid materials, equipment and facilities

28   When the assessment of first-aid requirements has been completed, the employer should provide the materials, equipment and facilities needed to ensure that the level of cover identified as necessary will be available to employees at all relevant times. This will include ensuring that first-aid equipment, suitably marked and easily accessible, is available in all places where working conditions require it.

First-aid containers

29   The minimum level of first-aid equipment is a suitably stocked and properly identified first-aid container. Every employer should provide for each work site at least one first-aid container supplied with a sufficient quantity of first-aid materials suitable for the particular circumstances.

30   First-aid containers should be easily accessible, and placed, if possible, near to hand washing facilities. Employers assessing the need for first-aid provision on large sites should consider providing more than one first-aid container. First-aid containers should protect first-aid items from dust and damp and should only be stocked with items useful for giving first aid. Tablets and medications should not be kept.

31   There is no mandatory list of items that should be included in a first-aid container. Employers should decide what to include in the first-aid container from information gathered during their assessment of first-aid needs. As a guide, where no special risk arises in the workplace, a minimum stock of first-aid items would normally be:

● a leaflet giving general guidance on first aid (for example HSE leaflet *Basic advice on first aid at work*[5]);

● 20 individually wrapped sterile adhesive dressings (assorted sizes), appropriate to the type of work (dressings may be of a detectable type for food handlers);

● two sterile eye pads;

6

- four individually wrapped triangular bandages (preferably sterile);

- six safety pins;

- six medium sized individually wrapped sterile unmedicated wound dressings - approximately 12 cm x 12 cm;

- two large sterile individually wrapped unmedicated wound dressings - approximately 18 cm x 18 cm;

- one pair of disposable gloves.

This is a suggested contents list only; equivalent but different items will be considered acceptable.

32   The contents of first-aid containers should be examined frequently and should be restocked as soon as possible after use. Sufficient supplies should be held in a back-up stock on site. Care should be taken to discard items safely after the expiry date has passed.

33   All first-aid containers must be identified by a white cross on a green background[6].

Additional first-aid materials and equipment

34   The assessment may conclude that there is a need for additional materials and equipment, for example scissors, adhesive tape, disposable aprons, individually wrapped moist wipes. These may be kept in the first-aid container if there is room. But they may be stored separately as long as they are available for use if required.

35   In particular circumstances the assessment might identify a need for items such as protective equipment, in case, for example, first aiders have to enter dangerous atmospheres; or blankets to protect casualties from the elements. These additional items should be securely stored near the first-aid container, in the first-aid room or in the hazard area, as appropriate. It is important that access to these items is restricted to people trained in their use.

36   Where mains tap water is not readily available for eye irrigation, at least a litre of sterile water or sterile normal saline (0.9%) in sealed, disposable containers should be provided. Once the seal has been broken, the containers should not be kept for reuse. The container should not be used after the expiry date.

Travelling first-aid kits

37   First-aid kits for travelling workers would typically contain:

- a leaflet giving general guidance on first aid (for example HSE leaflet *Basic advice on first aid at work*[5]);

- six individually wrapped sterile adhesive dressings;

- one large sterile unmedicated dressing - approximately 18 cm x 18 cm;

- two triangular bandages;

- two safety pins;

- individually wrapped moist cleansing wipes;

- one pair of disposable gloves.

This is a suggested contents list only; equivalent but different items will be considered acceptable. As with first-aid containers, the contents of kits should be kept stocked from the back-up stock at the home site.

First-aid rooms

38   Employers should provide a suitable first-aid room or rooms where the assessment of first-aid needs identifies this as necessary. The first-aid room(s) should contain essential first-aid facilities and equipment, be easily accessible to stretchers and be clearly signposted and identified. If possible, the room(s) should be reserved exclusively for giving first aid.

39   A first-aid room or rooms will usually be necessary in establishments with high risks, such as shipbuilding firms, chemical industries or large construction sites and in larger premises at a distance from medical services. A designated person should be given responsibility for the room.

40   To be effective, first-aid rooms should:

- be large enough to hold a couch, with enough space at each side for people to work, a desk, a chair and any necessary additional equipment;

- have washable surfaces and adequate heating, ventilation, and lighting;

- be kept clean, tidy, accessible and available for use at all times when employees are at work;

- be positioned as near as possible to a point of access for transport to hospital;

- display a notice on the door advising of the names, locations and, if appropriate, telephone extensions of first aiders and how to contact them.

41   Typical examples of the facilities and equipment a first-aid room may contain are:

- a sink with hot and cold running water;

- drinking water and disposable cups;

- soap and paper towels;

- a store for first-aid materials;

- foot-operated refuse containers, lined with disposable yellow clinical waste bags or a container suitable for the safe disposal of clinical waste;

- a couch with waterproof protection and clean pillows and blankets;

- a chair;

- a telephone or other communication equipment;

- a record book for recording incidents where first aid has been given (see paragraphs 56-57).

42   If the first-aid room(s) cannot be reserved exclusively for giving first aid, employers need to take care that the first-aid facilities can be made available quickly if necessary. For example, they should consider the implications of whether:

● the activities usually carried out in the room can be stopped immediately in an emergency;

● the furnishings and equipment can be moved easily and quickly to a position that will not interfere with giving first aid;

● the storage arrangements for first-aid furnishings and equipment allow them to be made available quickly when necessary.

43   The room(s) must be clearly signposted and identified by white lettering or symbols on a green background[6].

First-aid personnel

First aiders

44   Where the first-aid assessment identifies a need for people to be available for rendering first aid, the employer should ensure that they are provided in sufficient numbers and at appropriate locations to enable first aid to be administered without delay should the occasion arise. Where 50 or more people are employed, at least one such person should be provided unless the assessment justifies otherwise.

45   *Numbers.* The assessment (see paragraphs 4-27) will help employers to decide how many first aiders they need. There are no hard and fast rules on exact numbers since employers will have to form a judgement taking into consideration all the essential circumstances of that particular organisation or worksite. For example, a small organisation with comparatively low health and safety risks may not need a first aider (but will need an appointed person - see paragraphs 58-61). On the other hand, where an activity carries a high risk to health or safety and the workforce is spread across a number of work areas, at least one first aider might be needed in each separate work area, in addition to those at the main site.

46   When you have completed the assessment checklist in Appendix 1, look at Table 1. Table 1 offers suggestions on how many first aiders or appointed persons might be needed in relation to categories of risk and number of employees. The details in the table are suggestions only - they are not definitive, nor are they a legal requirement. It is for employers to assess their first-aid needs in the light of their particular circumstances.

47   *Selection.* The selection of first aiders depends on a number of factors, including an individual's:

● reliability, disposition and communication skills;

● aptitude and ability to absorb new knowledge and learn new skills;

● ability to cope with stressful and physically demanding emergency procedures;

● normal duties. These should be such that they may be left to go immediately and rapidly to an emergency.

Table 1 Suggested numbers of first-aid personnel to be available at all times people are at work, based on assessments of risk and number of workers

Where there are special circumstances, such as remoteness from emergency medical services, shiftwork, or sites with several separate buildings, there may need to be more first-aid personnel than set out below. Increased provision will be necessary to cover for absences.

Category of risk	Numbers employed at any location	Suggested number of first-aid personnel
Lower risk eg shops, offices, libraries	Fewer than 50	At least one appointed person
	50-100	At least one first aider
	More than 100	One additional first aider for every 100 employed
Medium risk eg light engineering and assembly work, food processing, warehousing	Fewer than 20	At least one appointed person
	20-100	At least one first aider for every 50 employed (or part thereof)
	More than 100	One additional first aider for every 100 employed
Higher risk eg most construction, slaughterhouse, chemical manufacture, extensive work with dangerous machinery or sharp instruments	Fewer than 5	At least one appointed person
	5-50	At least one first aider
	More than 50	One additional first aider for every 50 employed
	Where there are hazards for which additional first-aid skills are necessary	In addition, at least one first aider trained in the specific emergency action

48   *Qualifications and training.* Before taking up first-aid duties, a first aider must hold a valid certificate of competence in first aid at work, issued by an organisation whose training and qualifications are approved by HSE. Information on all the first aid at work training organisations approved by HSE is available from HSE's First Aid Approvals and Monitoring Section (see Appendix 3).

49   Training courses offer a basic curriculum in a range of first-aid competencies needed in any workplace. These competencies are listed in Appendix 2. When arranging training, employers should let the training organisation know of any particular hazards at work so that, if possible, the training can be tailored to their needs.

50   Special additional training may be necessary to cover less common risks so that first aiders can cope with particular problems. For example, more in-depth, specific training would be advisable in cases where first aid may need to be given because of risks from hydrofluoric acid or work in confined spaces.

51   This training may be undertaken as an extension to the basic training or as a separate course and does not need the approval of HSE. The standard certificate may be endorsed to verify that special hazard training has been received.

52   Guidance for training organisations on the standards and requirements for approval of training is given in a separate HSE publication[7].

53   As first aid at work certificates are only valid for the length of time HSE decides (currently three years), employers need to arrange refresher training with re-testing of competence before certificates expire. If a certificate expires, the individual will have to undertake a full course of training to be re-established as a first aider. However, employers can arrange for first aiders to attend a refresher course up to three months before the expiry date of their certificate. The new certificate will then take effect from the date of expiry. Employers may wish to keep a record of first aiders and certification dates to assist them with the timely arrangement of refresher training.

54   Employers should encourage first aiders to arrange a programme of self-directed revision in order to maintain their first-aid skills, and, where possible, should allocate them time to do this.

55   To develop their knowledge, first aiders may on occasions need further advice associated with first aid. Employers should ensure that first aiders are aware of suitable sources of advice, such as workplaces with occupational health services or organisations whose training and qualifications are approved by HSE.

56   *Records.* It is good practice for employers to provide first aiders and appointed persons with a book in which to record incidents which require their attendance. Where there are a number of first aiders working for a single employer, it would be advisable for one central book to be used, though this would not be practicable on larger, well spread-out sites. The information to be entered would include:

● date, time and place of incident;

● name and job of the injured or ill person;

● details of the injury/illness and what first aid was given;

● what happened to the person immediately afterwards (for example went home, went back to work, went to hospital);

● name and signature of the first aider or person dealing with the incident.

57   The information kept can help the employer identify accident trends and possible areas for improvement in the control of health and safety risks. It can be used for reference in future first-aid needs assessments. Such records may also be helpful for insurance and investigative purposes. This record book is not the same as the statutory accident book, though the two might be combined.

Appointed persons

58   Where an employer's assessment of first-aid needs identifies that a first aider is not necessary, the minimum requirement on an employer is to appoint a person to take charge of the first-aid arrangements, including looking after the equipment and facilities and calling the emergency services when required. Arrangements should be made for an appointed person to be available to undertake these duties at all times when people are at work.

59   Even in organisations with comparatively low health and safety risks where first aiders are considered unnecessary, there is always a possibility of accident or sudden illness. It is important, therefore, that someone is always available to take immediate action, such as calling an ambulance. Employers must, in the absence of first aiders, appoint a person for this purpose, though appointed persons are not necessary where there is an adequate number of first aiders.

60   It should be remembered that appointed persons are not first aiders and so should not attempt to give first aid for which they have not been trained. However, as the appointed person is required to look after the first-aid equipment and should ideally know how to use it, employers are strongly advised to consider the need for emergency first-aid training for appointed persons. Courses normally last four hours and cover the following topics:

● what to do in an emergency;

● cardio-pulmonary resuscitation;

● first aid for the unconscious casualty;

● first aid for the wounded or bleeding.

HSE approval is not required for this training.

61   The Regulations provide for a person to be appointed to provide emergency cover in the absence of first aiders but only where the absence is due to exceptional, unforeseen and temporary circumstances. Absences such as annual leave do not count. Remember that if the assessment calls for first aiders to be provided, they should be available whenever the need arises.

Duty of employer to inform his employees of the arrangements made in connection with first-aid

An employer shall inform his employees of the arrangements that have been made in connection with the provision of first-aid, including the location of equipment, facilities and personnel.

Information for employees

62   First-aid arrangements operate efficiently in an emergency only where they are known, understood, and accepted by everyone in the workplace. One way to achieve this is to set up procedures for informing staff in consultation with employees or safety representatives. The procedures should detail first-aid provision and explain how employees will be told the location of first-aid equipment, facilities and personnel. The procedures should also identify who will provide relevant first-aid information to new and transferred employees.

63   A simple method of keeping employees informed is by displaying first-aid notices. The information needs to be clear and easily understood by all employees. Employers should ensure that those with reading and language difficulties are also kept informed. For example:

● visually impaired employees could be informed by tape recorded messages or communications in Braille;

● employees with language difficulties could be informed by means of translated first-aid notices.

64   Notices must be designed and worded carefully to ensure that the information is put across effectively to employees. At least one notice in a prominent position at each site, including the base for travelling employees, should give enough opportunity for employees to see the information.

65   The inclusion of first-aid information in induction training will help ensure that new employees are made aware of the first-aid arrangements.

Duty of self-employed person to provide first-aid equipment

A self-employed person shall provide, or ensure that there is provided, such equipment, if any, as is adequate and appropriate in the circumstances to enable him to render first-aid to himself while he is at work.

Duties of self-employed persons

66   The systematic approach to assessment, set out in paragraphs 4-27 above, may also be valid for deciding how much first-aid provision is needed by the self-employed. Those who carry out comparatively low risk activities (for example clerical work) in their own homes would not be expected to provide first-aid equipment beyond their normal domestic needs.

67   Where the self-employed work on premises under the control of an employer or with other self-employed workers, they are each responsible for making their own first-aid provision. As indicated in paragraph 21, however, joint arrangements can be made with other occupiers to provide common cover.

Power to grant exemptions*

(1)   Subject to paragraph (2), the Health and Safety Executive may, by a certificate in writing, exempt any person or class of persons, from any of the requirements imposed by these Regulations, and any such exemption may be granted subject to conditions and to a limit of time and may be revoked at any time.

(2)   The Executive shall not grant any such exemption unless, having regard to the circumstances of the case, and in particular to -

(a)   the conditions, if any, which it proposes to attach to the exemption, and

(b)   any other requirements imposed by or under any enactment which apply to the case,

it is satisfied that the health, safety and welfare of employees and self-employed persons and the health and safety of other persons who are likely to be affected by the exemption will not be prejudiced in consequence of it.

Cases where these Regulations do not apply

These Regulations shall not apply -

(a)   where the Diving Operations at Work Regulations 1981[a] apply;

(b)   where the Merchant Shipping (Medical Scales) (Fishing Vessels) Regulations 1974[b] apply;

(c)   where the Merchant Shipping (Medical Stores) Regulations 1986[c] apply;

(d)   on vessels which are registered outside the United Kingdom;

(e)   [d]

* Regulation 24 of the Management of Health and Safety at Work Regulations 1999 revokes the Health and Safety Executive's powers to grant exemptions from the Health and Safety (First-Aid) Regulations 1981.

13

Regulation

7

    (f)   *in respect of the armed forces of the Crown and any force to which any provision of the Visiting Forces Act 1952[(e)] applies;*

    (g)   *where the Offshore Installations and Pipeline Works (First-Aid) Regulations 1989[(f)] apply.*

(a)   *SI 1981/399.*
(b)   *SI 1974/1192.*
(c)   *SI 1986/14.*
(d)   *Paragraph (e) is revoked by the Management and Administration of Safety and Health of Mines Regulations 1993, SI 1993 No 1897, regulation 44 (1), (2)(a), in so far as it applies to mines and mining operations.*
(e)   *SI 1952 c.67.*
(f)   *SI 1989/1671.*

Regulation 8

Application to mines

Regulation

8

    (1)   *Subject to Paragraph (2), in their application to mines, Regulation 3 and 4 shall have effect as if the owner of the mine were the employer and as if all persons for the time being employed at the mine were his employees.*

    (2)   *Paragraphs (3) and (4) of Regulation 3 shall not apply in relation to mines.*

Regulation 9

Application offshore

Regulation

9

    Subject to Regulation 7, these Regulations shall apply to and in relation to any premises or activity to or in relation to which sections 1 to 59 of the Health and Safety at Work etc. Act 1974 apply by virtue of Articles 6 and 7(a), (b) and (d) of the Health and Safety at Work etc. Act 1974 (Application outside Great Britain) Order 1977[(a)] (which relate respectively to mines extending beyond Great Britain and to certain activities concerning vessels and construction works in territorial waters).

(a)   *Revoked and replaced by SI/1995/263*

Regulation 10

Repeals, revocations and modification

Regulation

10

    (1)   *The enactments mentioned in column (1) of Schedule 1 are hereby repealed to the extent specified opposite thereto in column (3) of that Schedule.*

    (2)   *The Orders and Regulations mentioned in column (1) of Schedule 2 are hereby revoked to the extent specified opposite thereto in column (3) of that Schedule.*

Repeals

Regulation 10(1)

(1) Short title	(2) Chapter	(3) Extent of repeal
The Mines and Quarries Act 1954.	1954 c. 70; relevant amending instrument is SI 1974/2013.	In section 115, the words "section ninety-one (save in so far as it relates to persons employed below ground)" and in paragraph (a) the words "and ninety-one".
The Agriculture (Safety, Health and Welfare Provisions) Act 1956.	1956 c. 49.	Section 6(1) and (4).
The Factories Act 1961.	1961 c. 34.	Section 61.
The Offices, Shops and Railway Premises Act 1963.	1963 c. 41.	Section 24.

Revocations

Regulation 10(2)

(1) Regulations or Order	(2) Reference	(3) Extent of revocation
The Wool, Goat-Hair and Camel-Hair Regulations 1905.	SR & O 1905/1293.	Regulation 15.
The Horsehair Regulations 1907.	SR & O 1907/984.	Regulation 9(d).
The Ambulance and First-Aid Arrangements at Blast Furnaces, Copper Mills, Iron Mills, Foundries and Metal Works Order 1917.	SR & O 1917/1067; amended by SR & O 1925/863 and SI 1961/2434.	The whole Order.
The Saw Mills and Wood-working Factories Welfare (Ambulance and First Aid) Order 1918.	SR & O 1918/1489; amended by SR & O 1925/864 and SI 1961/2434.	The whole Order.
The Hides and Skins Regulations 1921.	SR & O 1921/2076.	Regulation 1.
The Chemical Works Regulations 1922.	SR & O 1922/731; relevant amending instruments are SI 1961/2435, 1981/16.	Regulations 10(a), 12, 13, 14 and 17(2)(g).

(1) Regulations or Order	(2) Reference	(3) Extent of revocation
Order dated 24th August 1925 revoking provisions in the Ambulance and First-Aid Arrangements at Blast Furnaces, Copper Mills, Iron Mills, Foundries and Metal Works Order 1917.	SR & O 1925/863.	The whole Order.
Order dated 24th August 1925 revoking provisions in the Saw Mills and Woodworking Factories Welfare (Ambulance and First Aid) Order 1918.	SR & O 1925/864.	The whole Order.
The Herring Curing (Scotland) Welfare Order 1926.	SR & O 1926/535; to which there are amendments not relevant to these Regulations.	Articles 3 and 4.
The Herring Curing Welfare Order 1927.	SR & O 1927/813, amended by SI 1960/1690.	Articles 3 and 4.
The Oil Cake Welfare Order 1929.	SR & O 1929/534.	Article 7.
The Docks Regulations 1934.	SR & O 1934/279, to which there are amendments not relevant to these Regulations.	Regulations 4 to 8.
The Clay Works (Welfare) Special Regulations 1948.	SI 1948/1547.	Regulation 7 and the Schedule.
The Miscellaneous Mines (General) Regulations 1956.	SI 1956/1778.	Regulation 71.
The Quarries (General) Regulations 1956.	SI 1956/1780.	Regulation 38.
The Agriculture (First Aid) Regulations 1957.	SI 1957/940.	The whole Regulations.
The First-aid Boxes in Factories Order 1959.	SI 1959/906; relevant amending instrument is SI 1961/1250.	The whole Order.
The Docks (First-aid Boxes) Order 1959.	SI 1959/2081.	The whole Order.
The First-aid (Standard of Training) Order 1960.	SI 1960/1612; relevant amending instrument is SI 1961/1250.	The whole Order.
The First-aid (Revocation) Regulations 1960.	SI 1960/1690.	The whole Regulations.
The First-aid Boxes (Miscellaneous Industries) Order 1960.	SI 1960/1691.	The whole Order.
The Shipbuilding and Ship-repairing Regulations 1960.	SI 1960/1932, to which there are amendments not relevant to these Regulations.	Regulation 79 and Schedule 3.

2

(1) Regulations or Order	(2) Reference	(3) Extent of revocation
The Railway Running Sheds Order 1961.	SI 1961/1250.	Paragraphs 8 and 9 of the Schedule.
The Blast Furnaces and Saw Mills Ambulance (Amendment) Regulations 1961.	SI 1961/2434.	The whole Regulations.
The Chemical Works Ambulance (Amendment) Regulations 1961.	SI 1961/2435.	The whole Regulations.
The Docks (Training in First-aid) Regulations 1962.	SI 1962/241.	The whole Regulations.
The Offices, Shops and Railway Premises First Aid Order 1964.	SI 1964/970; relevant amending instrument is SI 1974/1943.	The whole Order.
The Offices and Shops in Factories (First Aid) Regulations 1964.	SI 1964/1321.	The whole Regulations.
The Offices at Building Operations &c. (First Aid) Regulations 1964.	SI 1964/1322.	The whole Regulations.
The Offices in Electrical Stations (First Aid) Regulations 1964.	SI 1964/1323.	The whole Regulations.
The Information for Employees Regulations 1965.	SI 1965/307.	Paragraph 26 of the Schedule.
The Construction (Health and Welfare) Regulations 1966.	SI 1966/95, amended by SI 1974/209.	In Regulation 3(2), the words from "'certificate in first-aid' does not" to "or over" and from "'training organisation'" to "of these Regulations". In Regulation 4(2), the figures "5, 8, 9". Regulations 5 to 10. The Schedule.
The Ionising Radiations (Unsealed Radioactive Substances) Regulations 1968.	SI 1968/780; to which there are amendments not relevant to these Regulations.	Regulation 44(2).
The Abstract of Factories Act Order 1973.	SI 1973/7.	Paragraph 39 of Schedule 1.
The Factories Act General Register Order 1973.	SI 1973/8.	Part 7 of Schedule 1 and Part 5 of Schedule 2.
The Construction (Health and Welfare) (Amendment) Regulations 1974.	SI 1974/209.	The whole Regulations.
The Offices, Shops and Railway Premises Act 1963 (Repeals and Modifications) Regulations 1974.	SI 1974/1943.	Regulation 3(2).
The Chemical Works (Metrication) Regulations 1981.	SI 1981/16.	All entries in the Schedule relating to Regulation 12 of the Chemical Works Regulations 1922.

Assessment of first-aid needs checklist

The minimum first-aid provision for each work site is:

- a suitably stocked first-aid container (see paragraphs 29-33);

- a person appointed to take charge of first-aid arrangements (see paragraphs 58-61);

- information for employees on first-aid arrangements (see paragraphs 62-65).

This checklist will help you assess whether you need to make any additional provision.

Aspects to consider	*Impact on first-aid provision*
1 What are the risks of injury and ill health arising from the work as identified in your risk assessment? (see paragraphs 10-11)	If the risks are significant you may need to employ first aiders.
2 Are there any specific risks, eg working with: – hazardous substances; – dangerous tools; – dangerous machinery; – dangerous loads or animals? (see paragraph 12)	You will need to consider: – specific training for first aiders; – extra first-aid equipment; – precise siting of first-aid equipment; – informing emergency services; – first-aid room.
3 Are there parts of your establishment where different levels of risk can be identified (eg in a University with research laboratories)? (see paragraph 13)	You will probably need to make different levels of provision in different parts of the establishment.
4 Are large numbers of people employed on site? (see paragraph 14 and Table 1)	You may need to employ first aiders to deal with the higher probability of an accident.
5 What is your record of accidents and cases of ill health? What type are they and where did they happen? (see paragraph 15)	You may need to: – locate your provision in certain areas; – review the contents of the first-aid box.
6 Are there inexperienced workers on site, or employees with disabilities or special health problems? (see paragraph 16)	You will need to consider: – special equipment; – local siting of equipment.
7 Are the premises spread out, eg are there several buildings on the site or multi-floor buildings? (see paragraph 17)	You will need to consider provision in each building or on several floors.
8 Is there shiftwork or out-of-hours working? (see paragraph 18)	Remember that there needs to be first-aid provision at all times people are at work.
9 Is your workplace remote from emergency medical services? (see paragraph 19)	You will need to: – inform local medical services of your location; – consider special arrangements with the emergency services.

Aspects to consider	Impact on first-aid provision
10 Do you have employees who travel a lot or work alone? (see paragraph 20)	You will need to: – consider issuing personal first-aid kits and training staff in their use; – consider issuing personal communicators to employees.
11 Do any of your employees work at sites occupied by other employers? (see paragraph 21)	You will need to make arrangements with the other site occupiers.
12 Do you have any work experience trainees? (see paragraph 24)	Remember that your first-aid provision must cover them.
13 Do members of the public visit your premises? (see paragraph 25)	You have no legal responsibilities for non-employees, but HSE strongly recommends you include them in your first-aid provision.
14 Do you have employees with reading or language difficulties? (see paragraph 63)	You will need to make special arrangements to give them first-aid information.

Don't forget that first aiders and appointed persons take leave and are often absent from the premises for other reasons. You must appoint sufficient people to cover these absences to enable first-aid personnel to be available at all times people are at work.

First-aid competencies (paragraph 49)

On completion of training successful candidates need to be able to apply the following competencies:

(a) the ability to act safely, promptly and effectively when an emergency occurs at work;

(b) the ability to administer cardio-pulmonary resuscitation (CPR) promptly and effectively;

(c) the ability to administer first aid safely, promptly and effectively to a casualty who is unconscious;

(d) the ability to administer first aid safely, promptly and effectively to a casualty who is wounded or bleeding;

(e) the ability to administer first aid safely, promptly and effectively to a casualty who:

- has been burned or scalded;

- is suffering from an injury to bones, muscles or joints;

- is suffering from shock;

- has an eye injury;

- may be poisoned;

- has been overcome by gas or fumes;

(f) the ability to transport a casualty safely as required by the circumstances of the workplace;

(g) the ability to recognise common major illnesses and take appropriate action;

(h) the ability to recognise minor illnesses and take appropriate action;

(i) the ability to maintain simple factual records and provide written information to a doctor or hospital if required.

Students will also be required to demonstrate knowledge and understanding of the principles of first aid at work, in particular of:

(a) the importance of personal hygiene in first-aid procedures;

(b) the legal framework for first-aid provision at work;

(c) the use of first-aid equipment provided in the workplace;

(d) the role of the first aider in emergency procedures.

Further information

Information on organisations approved by HSE to run first aid at work training courses is available from HSE, First Aid Approvals and Monitoring Section, Grove House, Skerton Road, Manchester M16 0RB Tel: 0161 952 8322

For general enquiries on first aid at work ring HSE's Infoline Tel: 08701 545500 Fax: 02920 859260 e-mail: hseinformationservices@natbrit.com or write to HSE Information Services, Caerphilly Business Park, Caerphilly CF83 3GG. You can also visit HSE's website: www.hse.gov.uk

References and further reading

References

1   *First aid at mines. Health and Safety (First-Aid) Regulations 1981. Approved Code of Practice* L43 1993 HSE Books ISBN 0 7176 0617 1

2   *Management of health and safety at work. Management of Health and Safety at Work Regulations 1999. Approved Code of Practice and guidance* L21 (Second edition) 2000 HSE Books ISBN 0 7176 2488 9

3   *Five steps to risk assessment* Leaflet INDG163(rev1) 1998 HSE Books (single copy free or in priced packs of 10, ISBN 0 7176 1565 0)

4   *The Health and Safety (Training for Employment) Regulations 1990* SI 1990/1380 The Stationery Office ISBN 0 11 004380 4

5   *Basic advice on first aid at work* Leaflet INDG347 HSE Books 2002 (single copy free or priced packs of 20, ISBN 0 7176 2261 4)

6   *Safety signs and signals. The Health and Safety (Safety Signs and Signals) Regulations 1996. Guidance on Regulations* L64 1996 HSE Books ISBN 0 7176 0870 0

7   *The training of first-aid at work. A guide to training and maintaining HSE approval* HSG212 (Second edition) HSE Books 2000 ISBN 0 7176 1896 X

Further reading

First aid at work: Your questions answered Leaflet INDG214 HSE Books 1997 (single copy free or priced packs of 15 ISBN 0 7176 1074 8)

Printed and published by the Health and Safety Executive

C50   6/04